It's been another busy year here at the CCLaP blog, with reviewers Karl Wolff, Chris Schahfer and Jason Pettus turning in a total of 89 write-ups in 2015; and now here is our annual look at our favorite 40 of those, broken down into a series of specialized reports...

Best of the Best
Karl Wolff's Favorites
Chris Schahfer's Favorites
Jason Pettus' Favorites
The CCLaP Guilty Pleasure Awards

Our thanks to all of you for continuing to come back here to the blog each day, year in and out, to see the latest of what we've had to say about the books we've been reading. We look forward to bringing you another active year of critical essays in 2016.

The Year In Books 2015

From the web pages of the Chicago Center for Literature and Photography

Printed and distributed by the Chicago Center for
Literature and Photography. *First paperback edition,
first printing: December 2015.*

ISBN: 978-1-939987-42-6

Best of the Best

Other lists coming later this week will feature each individual CCLaP reviewer's personal favorite reads of the year, and of course don't forget that we encourage you not to read too much into numerical scores here in the first place (one person's sci-fi masterpiece is another person's eye-rolling steampunk trainwreck). But if you were to put together a master list combining all the highest scoring books by all of our staff reviewers over the course of 2015, that list would look like the following, arranged alphabetically by title and with each reviewer's initials appearing at the end (KW: Karl Wolff; CS: Chris Schahfer; JP: Jason Pettus).

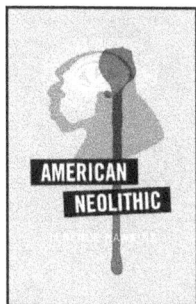

American Neolithic, by Terence Hawkins (C&R Press). I must confess, I was expecting little more than Just Another Ho-Hum Academic Novel when this first arrived, penned by the founding director of the Yale Writers' Conference; so imagine my surprise when this turned out to not only be a hauntingly poetic look at a pulpy question straight from speculative genre fiction ("What if neanderthals still existed in our modern world?"), but also a smart alt-history novel about what our nation might look like if the Tea Party wins the next Presidential election. Like the best of Michael Chabon or Rick Moody, this is a blend of genre writing and fine-art literature for those who demand only the best writers in America writing at the top of their game; and in a different age this book would've come out with great fanfare from a place like Random House and won the Pulitzer Prize, not from an obscure small press where it received almost no attention. This IS one of the best books you will read this year, so don't delay in picking up a copy. (JP)

The Argonauts, by Maggie Nelson (Graywolf Press). People wonder what poststructuralist theory and semiotics have to do with them. Maggie Nelson's got an answer. In this brilliant memoir-study-love letter about her transgender partner, she recounts her experience with a more self-defined model of gender. She also calls out academia as a boy's club, rips into the Christian right, tells the story of her first child's birth, meditates on Greek mythology, and somehow finds the time for plenty of deadpan humor. All of this in one hundred fifty pages. For fear of hyperbole, an incredible achievement. (CS)

Between the World and Me, by Ta-Nehisi Coates (Spiegel & Grau). Yeah, I know. It was everyone's favorite book of 2015, the one everyone agreed on, etc. Can you blame me for loving this so much, though? Coates is a guy with a lot to say, both about race and basic human dignity, and his way of saying it is a great combination of eloquent and fiery, not to mention void of easy answers. If that weren't enough for you, the man's brilliant storytelling skills are exemplified in episodes about his high school and college years. One for believers in the David Foster Wallace dictum that great literature should disturb the comforted and comfort the disturbed. (CS)

A Curious Man, by Neal Thompson (Three Rivers Press). The life and times of Robert "Believe It or Not!" Ripley, a boy from hardscrabble rural California who became a cartoonist. He later spun his cartooning into one of the first multimedia empires. (KW)

Gutshot, by Amelia Gray (FSG Originals). People keep calling Amelia Gray's fiction "creepy," "grotesque," and "full of stories about giant snakes who split towns in half" like it's a bad thing. Yet Amelia's third collection and fourth book overall proves she's got it together, even if her books aren't fun little skips through fields of daisies. Instead, these stories are as bizarre and claustrophobic—and as frequently hilarious—as earlier work like *AM/PM*, except now her bizarre world is starting to look more and more like a real place. It might be a few years before she follows this one up, but I can't wait for what she plans to do next. (CS)

The Last Bookaneer, by Matthew Pearl (Penguin Press). Definitely not for everyone—there are plenty of complaints about this novel online, in fact—the reason this historical thriller made my particular Best Of The Best list is from the super-fetishistic nature of its subject matter, seemingly perfectly tailored exactly for me; it's set in the world of Victorian "bookaneers," back when copyright laws had just been invented in the US and the UK but before either country recognized the legality of the other's, when a publisher could make a lot of money by swiping a well-known manuscript from the other country before the book had come out there, and romantic "literary pirates" could make a lot of money by being the swipers. A globetrotting tale that takes us from the smoky back alleys of London all the way to Robert Louis Stevenson's jungle mansion in Samoa, on top of everything else this is also a sneakily sly ode to contemporary paper books in an age of Kindles, as well as a pretty convincing argument for why all of us should be collectors of rare first editions. (JP)

Muscle Cars, by Stephen G. Eoannou (Santa Fe Writers Project). A wondrous, accessible short story collection focuses on the Greek-American community in upstate New York. It is also a powerful rumination about how men see themselves in this time of perpetual war and drastic social change. (KW)

Pepperpot: Best New Stories from the Caribbean (Peepal Tree Press / Akashic Books). I always love opportunities to read about other cultures that are sometimes far different than my own; and this particular one (a co-branding effort from our pals at Akashic Books) is especially great, because it presents not just a stereotypical sun-drenched, brightly colored cornucopia of happy Caribbean natives like many other region-boostering anthologies might, but goes out of its way to include stories about white collar criminals, suburban middle-class families, and other pieces that show off the incredible diversity of this complex series of islands. If you're looking for a book on Caribbean culture that's not some magical-realism Gabriel Garcia Marquez ripoff, this is the anthology for you. (JP)

The Peripheral, by William Gibson (G.P. Putnam's Sons / Penguin. The inventor of cyberpunk, who lately has been writing a series of present-day thrillers, returns to science-fiction for the first time in a decade, and the results are hugely entertaining. A dual story that partly takes place thirty years from now, and partly another seventy years after that, Gibson gets to eat his cake here and have it too, turning in a look at such day-after-tomorrow fears as Western fascism, surveillance states, and 3D printing of illegal devices, but also getting to play in his far-future sandbox that he's such a master at, presenting us a series of head-exploding ideas about what a post-apocalyptic, rapidly depopulated and re-greened "living building" London might look like a century from now. Not his most cutting-edge book to be sure, but a great return to form that will keep both old fans and new very happy. (JP)

See You in the Morning, by Mairead Case (Featherproof Press). A small press gem for all you small press people. Humble as this book is, it's easily worthy of my number four slot. Coming-of-age stories have been beaten to death, yet Case manages to inject a lot of life into the genre's corpse. Her unnamed narrator passes through a confusing world with a voice that's just the right combination of sweet and confused. It's twee, sure, but whoever had a problem with twee? Likeable characters aren't everything in fiction, but I guarantee you will like this narrator by about the fourth or fifth page. (CS)

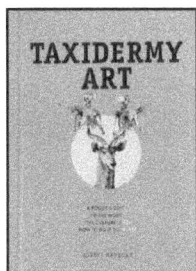

Taxidermy Art, by Robert Marbury (Artisan). Marbury, the founder of the Minnesota Association of Rogue Taxidermists, curates a collection of eccentric taxidermy. The art works challenge and question our relationship with death and the animal world, but in a kitschy, glorious, tongue-in-cheek manner. (KW)

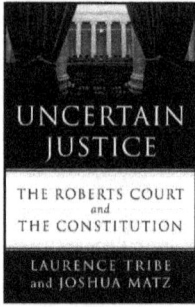

Uncertain Justice: The Roberts Court and the Constitution, by Laurence Tribe and Joshua Matz (Picador). Arguably one the best primers on the inner workings of the United States Supreme Court. Tribe and Matz team up to succinctly explain the opposing arguments and tricky decisions of the Roberts Court. All the greatest hits are here: gun control, abortion, free speech, healthcare, privacy, and presidential power. The challenge is discovering when both sides have valid arguments for a prickly legal dispute. (KW)

Karl Wolff's Favorites

Veteran CCLaP book reviewer Karl Wolff had a great year in 2015, publishing his latest book of critical essays (*The NSFW Files*) and finishing the writing of his next one after that (*American Odd*, coming in paperback form in 2016). Here's his look at his personally favorite five reads of this year.

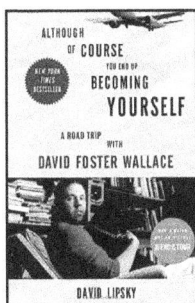

Although of Course You End Up Becoming Yourself: A Road Trip with David Foster Wallace, by David Lipsky (Broadway Books). The Jason Segel film *The End of the Tour* brought about a revival of interest in the late author David Foster Wallace. The book, like the film, traces David Lipsky's travels with DFW on a book tour for *Infinite Jest*. I enjoyed it because it showed another side of DFW, humanizing this innovative and daring author.

Cities of Empire: The British colonies and the creation of the urban world, by Tristram Hunt (Metropolitan Books/Henry Holt and Company). Profiling noteworthy urban developments from Boston to Liverpool to Hong Kong, *Cities of Empire* is a great read for architecture nerds. Hunt, a member of Parliament, investigates urban planning, architecture, politics, and anti-imperialist sentiment in a history that spans the globe.

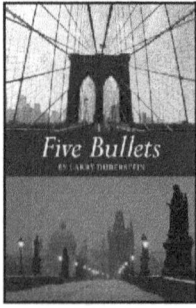

Five Bullets, by Larry Duberstein (Brimstone Corner Press). *Mad Men* meets *Titus Andronicus* in this immigrant story of midcentury New York City. The story bounces between past and present, Europe and America, Nazi death camps and corporate board rooms, capitalist achievement and cold-blooded revenge. It is a thriller unlike any other.

Predator: the Secret Origins of the Drone Revolution, by Richard Whittle (Henry Holt and Company). *Predator* tells the story of the development, military use, and legal limbo of the Predator drone. The gee-whiz technological development goes hand in hand with the legal miasma associated with drones. Whittle doesn't shy away from either, writing a balanced account of a controversial new technology.

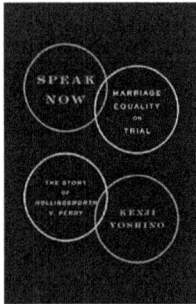

Speak Now: Marriage Speak Now: Marriage Equality on Trial, by Kenji Yoshino (Crown). Yoshino's legal history of the struggle for marriage equality is learned, accessible, and emotionally resonant. Regardless of where you stand on LGBT rights, this book offers a level-headed examination of both sides. An Asian-American gay man who married and has adopted two children, he also celebrated the recent Supreme Court ruling in favor of The Westboro Baptist Church. This might confound NPR leftists, but Yoshino embraced the opinion because the law is meant for all and the ruling was a triumph for free expression.

Chris Schahfer's Favorites

This was Chicagoan Chris Schahfer's first full year as a reviewer here at CCLaP, where among his general duties he also wrote the essay collection Stalking the Behemoth, coming in paperback form in 2016. Here's his personally favorite six reads of this year.

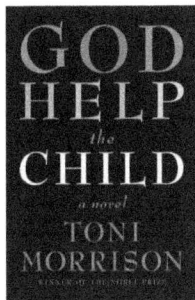

Best Otherwise Solid Book Spoiled By a Forced Ending: *God Help the Child*, by Toni Morrison (Albert A. Knopf, Inc.). Morrison's first book set in the contemporary period. This one expands her range a little, switching between first and third person narration effectively, and boasts typically spellbinding storytelling, some great character development, and Morrison's will to put her characters through hell. Then she decides that we need a happy ending that puts much too neat of a bow on the story, and I get off the boat. Come on, Toni Morrison. You can do better than this.

Best Book I Can't Review Because of Conflicts of Interest But Had a Good Time With Anyway: *Toughlahoma*, by Christian Tebordo (Rescue Press). Christian Tebordo's one of my professors, so I didn't feel comfortable reviewing this book. Still, it's a great read for any fans of strange fiction, full of puns, surreal Biblical references, dark humor, and as many storytelling modes as the guy could

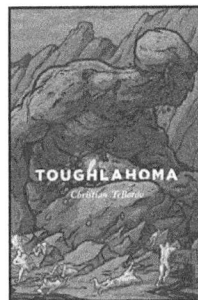

fit into a hundred pages. It might seem like a satire on Christianity, but I guarantee you it's a lot more nuanced and interesting than that. Suzanne Scanlon's fragmentary novel *Her Thirty-Seventh Year: An Index* also deserves mention in this category.

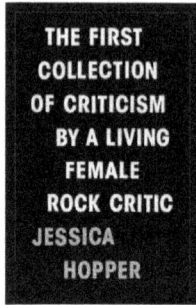

Best Book of Music Criticism That's Also a Memoir: *The First Collection of Criticism by a Living Female Rock Critic*, by Jessica Hopper (Featherproof Books). Like a lot of rock bands, a lot of rock criticism is better in theory than in practice. Not even the better stuff, like some of Lester Bangs' wild '70s writing, qualifies as literature. So why am I throwing this in the mix? Literature is about transferring an experience, and some of the best pieces in this collection, like Hopper's account of pretending to be a grunge fan in high school to get a boy's attention, transfer her experience of being a music fan to us readers. So I guess we can call it a memoir in the form of rock criticism.

Book That Would Make for a Good Movie: *Morning and Evening*, by Jon Fosse (Dalke Archive). I wasn't as into this book as a few of the others, but I'm pitching it in here anyway. Fosse is often compared to Beckett, but this novel's meditations on age, morality and metaphysics remind me more of Ingmar Bergman. It's one of those books that might translate better as a film. A good enough actor and a strong setting could bring this to life. I'm imagining a not-quite-right version of the real world, lots of fog and water, a slow rolling pace, and plenty of weird circular dialog with a comedic/philosophical bent. Someone get Max Von Sydow on the phone, because I think I've found his next starring role.

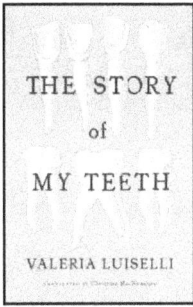

Best Book About Famous Authors' Teeth: *The Story of My Teeth*, by Valeria Luiselli (Coffee House Press). Luiselli's had a big couple of years lately. How better to keep that train rolling than with a comic novel about the teeth of the famous and a hilariously inflated auctioneer? This one was serialized, written in collaboration with workers at a juice factory, and it has a terrifying but hilarious sequence with clowns and a protagonist who's oddly likable despite his obvious narcissism. I like her ghostly 2013 novel *Faces in the Crowd* a little bit more, but this is one of those rare books that's as hilarious on the page as it is in theory.

Best Comedy About Soul-Crushing Lack of Fulfillment: *Jillian*, by Halle Butler (Curbside Splendor). Two main characters here: Megan, a 24-year-old who feels her friends are more successful than she is, and Jillian, an optimist despite her sad life. The two of them work at the same office and hate each other. You don't need me here to tell you that there's a lot of sadness under this book's surface, or that there are moments where it comes out in huge and almost unbearable rushes. Still, Butler's deadpan dialog and eye for the absurd makes it one of the funnier depictions of two people in crisis I've read.

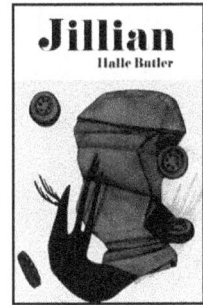

Jason Pettus' Favorites

CCLaP owner Jason Pettus had a busy year away from the center in 2015, starting and completing an intense "computer programming bootcamp" in Chicago in preparation for a day-job career change next year; but he still managed to squeeze in time to read and review around 50 books or so here at the blog. Here today is a look at his ten personally favorite titles of this year.

No Land's Man, by Aasif Mandvi (Chronicle Books). Actor, writer, and former *Daily Show* correspondent Aasif Mandvi's autobiography is a real treat, a funny and disarming look at one Muslim pop-culture nerd's forays into first British suburban culture and then '80s Florida. For those who only know this multi-disciplinary artist for his comedy, this heartfelt memoir will be a welcome surprise.

Victims, by Travis Jeppesen (ITNA Press). Our friends at ITNA Press are doing God's work these days, putting out a string of tough, challenging books that would otherwise not have a home; take this transgressive classic, for example, originally published in 2003 but long out of print, a difficult experimental read concerning both a woman who has fallen into a cult and her son's struggles decades

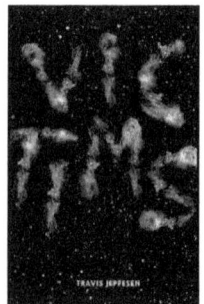

later to leave that cult. Not for everyone, but those who like these kinds of stories will absolutely love this one.

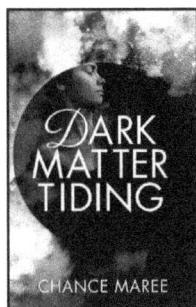

Dark Matter Tiding, by Chance Maree (Self-published). Although we've admittedly been having some problems with this subject in the last six months, there's also a very good reason why CCLaP wades through the increasing number of self-published novels we receive on a daily basis; and *Dark Matter Tiding* is a good example of that reason, a smart and thrilling sci-fi actioner that can easily hold its own against anything put out by Pyr or Orbit.

The Village: 400 Years of Beats and Bohemians, Radicals and Rogues—A History of Greenwich Village, by John Strausbaugh (Ecco/HarperCollins); and *Rebel Souls: Walt Whitman and America's First Bohemians*, by Justin Martin (Merloyd Lawrence Books / Da Capo Press / Perseus). Two great books came out this year about the same subject, which is why I'm lumping them into one write-up here: John Strausbaugh's *The Village* covers the entire history of New York's Greenwich Village neighborhood, which has existed now for almost 400 years and has been a home to bohemian artists almost that entire time; while Justin Martin's *Rebel Souls* looks at Greenwich Village just in the Victorian Age, when people like Walt Whitman made this one of the first-ever areas in American history to be friendly to gays and middle-class people of color. Together they give an illuminating portrait of this surprisingly progressive area of NYC, and present a whole new way for us to think about the normally repressed Victorian era.

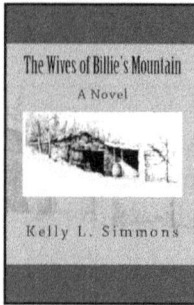

The Wives of Billie's Mountain, by Kelly L. Simmons (Self-published). Unfortunately CCLaP started to see a big problem arising with basement-press and self-published books in 2015—it's so technologically easy to publish a paperback anymore, there are just millions of crappy titles coming out these days, making it harder and harder to find the truly great ones lost in the mix—but thankfully a few of these much needed titles still came shining through this year. Here's one of them, a frontier story written in the style of Laura Ingalls Wilder, but based on the true tale of the multiple wives of a Mormon husband, who all had to go live secretly in nearby caves when the government started getting on their case about their polygamy.

The Poor Children, by April L. Ford (Santa Fe Writers Project). You think at first that this is going to be just another so-so social realist drama about rural children in crisis; but then it quickly turns a *lot* darker and weirder than that, an unholy baby made up of equal parts Bonnie Jo Campbell, Sam Shepard and Dennis Cooper. SWFP actually sent us a lot of great books this year, but this one was easily the best.

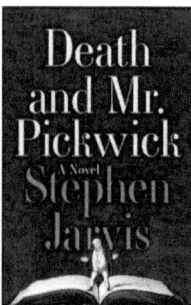

Death and Mr. Pickwick, by Stephen Jarvis (Farrar, Straus and Giroux). This won't be everyone's cup of tea, but I rather loved this overstuffed, deliberately formal-feeling contemporary historical novel, purporting to tell the "true story" of why the original illustrator of Charles Dickens' *The Pickwick Papers* killed himself just three chapters in, but in reality a sweeping and detail-obsessed look at what daily life in the early Victorian Age was actually like for most people.

You gotta already love Dickensian stories in order to love this; but if you do, this is a must-read.

Submission, by Michel Houellebecq (Farrar, Straus and Giroux). LOOK OUT! The intellectual world's most controversial author has published yet another instantly controversial intellectual novel, positing a France who in the next election (through a convoluted series of events) end up choosing the Muslim Brotherhood to run the country, looking at the mad rush among academic liberals to instantly renounce their decadent Western concepts of "democracy" and "marriage for love" and "equal rights for women" in order to curry favor with their new Islamic masters. A sneakily metaphorical indictment of how quickly France rolled over to the Nazis in World War Two, you stand a high chance of being offended by this take-no-prisoners story, the exact reason you should read it in the first place.

The Way Inn, by Will Wiles (Harper Perennial). A fantastic surrealist tale whose reading just squeaked in under this year's deadline, this short and powerful novel is sort of like Douglas Coupland (a sociological look at what bland suburban hotels say about us as a species) and sort of like David Lynch (in that there's a lot more quantum weirdness than first meets the eye to the particular bland hotel at the heart of our particular story). A book for fans of <i>Lost</i> and other such head-scratching, well-written oddness.

The CCLaP Guilty Pleasure Awards

CCLaP has a proud tradition now of closing each annual Year In Books report with the coveted Guilty Pleasure Awards -- books that we loved and want to bring to your attention again, but for one reason or another just don't quite qualify for the traditional "best-of" lists we've been posting here the rest of the week. As always, they're listed in alphabetical order by title, with the particular reviewer's initials at the end of each write-up (KW: Karl Wolff; JP: Jason Pettus).

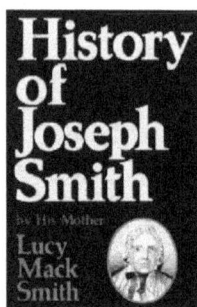

History of Joseph Smith by His Mother, by Lucy Mack Smith (Bookcraft). I'm a sucker for anything relating to Mormonism. Like Scientology, it is a strange new religion, very much American in origin. The autobiography of the Prophet Joseph Smith as told by his mother represents one of the weirdest literary products from Mormon culture. (KW)

Kooks: A Guide to the Outer Limits of Human Belief, by Donna Kossy (Feral House). A classic of the genre, Kooks explores the outer limits of human beliefs. Covering everything from junk science to conspiracy theories, Kossy plumbs the depths of the intellectually weird. It is an anthropological document, preserving the otherwise overlooked fringes of culture. (KW)

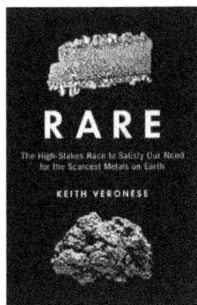

Rare: The High-Stakes Race to Satisfy Our Need for the Scarcest Metals on Earth, by Keith Veronese (Prometheus Books). A nonfiction scientific book about obscure metals in central Asia, one of the best reads of the year? Yes! But only if you can get into the NPR spirit of it all, which is why it made the Guilty Pleasure Awards instead of my favorites list. If you're not up for a wonky read on the finer points of mining, smelting, and Cold War history, this book is going to be a real drag; but if you are, you'll see how fascinating the subject of rare metals is about to be to our society, being responsible as they are for making most of our high-tech gadgets work, but with a finite supply that is dwindling away to nothing even as we speak. It's the scramble for the unmined deposits of this material in the former Soviet states that will fuel most of the ground wars we'll see in the 21st century, so do yourself a favor and read up on this interesting subject now before the tanks start rolling. (JP)

Sick Pack, by MP Johnson (JournalStone). A group of abs rebel against their Fabio-esque host in a mad bid for freedom in modern Los Angeles. Once again, MP Johnson brings a poignant emotional core to the otherwise bloody, violent, and profane genre of bizarro literature. (KW)

Something Good, Something Bad, Something Dirty: Stories, by Brian Alan Ellis (House of Vlad Productions). This short story collection scours the scummy denizens of all-night diners and trailer parks. By turns hilarious and horrifying, *Something Good, Something Bad, Something Dirty,* delves into the forgotten corners of our nation, exploring the lives of those passed over by the American Dream. (KW)

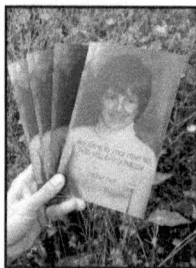

Welcome To Your New Life With You Being Happy, by Rachel Bell (Pioneers Press). Yes, I admit, I found this tiny book of tiny stories only okay when first reading it earlier this year; but I confess that Bell's work continues to grow on me as the months continue, helped quite a bit by following her drunken, comedic antics over at Facebook and elsewhere. I still contend that we haven't seen any truly great work from her yet, which is why this book is getting a Guilty Pleasure Award instead of being in my favorites list—you have to have a high tolerance for substance abuse, ironic worship of pop culture, and other undergraduate fixations in order to truly enjoy this particular volume—but certainly her sincere and sometimes heartfelt takes on such topics is far and away much better than the hipster parlor games of such contemporaries of hers as Tao Lin and Heiko Julien, which is why I'm excited to see what future work we'll be getting from Bell, instead of being filled with dread like when I think of so many other Millennial writers with cultish online followings. In the meantime, pick up this chapbook now, so that you too can one day proudly proclaim, "I was reading Rachel Bell long before all the mainstream douchebags were." (JP)

You're Never Weird On the Internet (Almost), by Felicia Day (Touchstone / Simon & Schuster). It's hard to call this truly one of the best books of the year—unlike her sharp, dark writing on the cult web series *The Guild*, this autobiography is often as cutesy-wootsy-tootsy as Grumpy Cat barfing a rainbow all over a unicorn's Hello Kitty collection—but that said, it's hard not to love

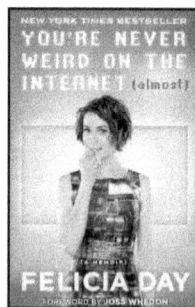

Felicia Day's memoir of growing up as a gifted child anyway, and especially the self-deprecating way she examines how the early online world of the 1990s gave her much-needed opportunities to brush up on normalization and socialization skills, just to have this medium turn her into a bonafide media celebrity and "geek sex symbol"

twenty years later. Not to mention, a specific part of this book is worth its purchase price alone, when she very soberly takes on the ugliness in recent years regarding the so-called "men's movement" in the online gaming world, and what it's like to try to live as a normal random human while being such a easy target for such people's hate; apart from the kawaii nature of so much of the rest of this book, the last couple of chapters are a serious, deliberately political and always passionate argument for why women's rights in the online world matter, and why basic respect for women is so hard to achieve in a community of a billion anonymous strangers who face no repercussions to their actions. (JP)

www.ingramcontent.com/pod-product-compliance
Lightning Source LLC
Chambersburg PA
CBHW020450030426
42337CB00014B/1494

If finding love is your deepest wish, then establishing a meaningful connection is the means to that end. The best way to achieve this is by knowing your compatibility needs and learning how to effectively communicate.

Tip: Aim to Make a Meaningful Connection

Expectation can be everything when you start this journey. Misplaced expectations can lead to hurt feelings and a bad experience. Going online to find love is too much pressure and can often cloud your judgment. If you are the type of person that has an active imagination and "falls in and out of love" easily, I would hold your horses and take a more practical approach to your online pursuits.

A meaningful connection happens after you've passed the phase of fluffy introductory conversations, gazed at their photos, discussed your deal breakers, verified the chemistry, and have shared a significant amount of time developing a friendship. A true friendship – not the superficial associations that we make on Facebook and other social networks, but one that can lead to a relationship. Connections like this stand out from your other matches and rise above the rest of the fillers. You are going to meet a lot of people online. This type of connection may be far and few between – but they're completely worth it.

{ 2 }

My Keep It Real Rule

Keep. It. Real. Yes, it sounds simple but it's the foundational rule for all of the other tips and recommendations that are discussed in this guide. There are three components to my Keep It Real Rule that should be considered in all interactions with your matches.

Keep Your Goal at the Forefront

"Are you looking for a travel buddy, friend, long-term relationship, or marriage?"

I never knew that a travel buddy could be an actual online status. If your reasoning for joining a dating site is to establish a friendship with a travel buddy, then your interactions, profile set up and level of communication, should be very different from someone who is in search of their life partner. You will receive a number of opportunities that can sway you from your goal, and it's important to keep your goal at the forefront of all your interactions. Keeping your goal doesn't mean that you lose sight of meeting new people, making a meaningful connection and doing your best to develop true friendships.

It's equally important to look at the goals written in your match's profile. This will help you to determine if you share the same objectives. Hold on to your goal as if it's a life preserver in a choppy body of water. It will keep you anchored amid the waves of expectation and the hard rocks of reality.

Be Your True Authentic Self

Being authentic may seem like a no-brainer. However, the internet seems to provide a blanket of comfort that allows users to be more or less of themselves. If you would not walk up to a strange woman and ask her how much she weighs or for her physical measurements, then you shouldn't do this online. Being authentic is being the everyday you.

If you love to tell jokes that only you seem to understand, then share one on your profile. All of our quirks and kinks make us special and unique. If you go to Comic Con, still dress up for Halloween and have an addiction to reality TV - cool! Show a picture of you dressed up on your profile page. If your happiness is centered on daily chants and meditation – super! Let your matches know. If you feel that you have a calling to save the Japanese beetle – great! Please share that on your profile. You really wouldn't want anyone to be surprised by that- and not in a good way. If this is the real you, then a true match will not be turned off by something that turns you on.

Bottom line: Be the real you the person will meet at the coffee shop or in a bookstore.

Expectation is created by what we say and do online. If you are giving someone an expectation that doesn't exist in the real world– then you are setting yourself up for failure and potentially a terrible experience for yourself or someone else. Why waste your energy and time pretending or putting on flares for people that may never like you? If there is something you don't like about yourself - then change. There may be some things we can't change about ourselves, such as a disability. Be sure to accept yourself so that others will also. Human perfection does not exist and we're all a work in progress. On the other hand, if you are interested in playing games, save the money you would spend on a dating site membership and purchase a few lives on Candy Crush. The universe will thank you in the long run. Online dating is for grown-ups, not kids!

Communicate Effectively

All the best of anything relational is built on good effective communication. The best business partnerships, the best marriages, the best friendships, the best contracts, even the best prenups – all have a foundation in good and effective communication. I'm using the word effective because it's a barometer that determines the outcome of the communication tools you use. Effective communication does not necessarily mean that you are in agreement or disagreement. It means that an understanding has taken place between the two parties. After you have flirted, chatted, messaged, texted, talked on the phone, maybe met once or twice, you really want to make sure that you are communicating in a way that provides you both with basic understandings.

Below is a list of ways you can communicate more effectively:

•**Discuss your preferred method of communication** (text, video, telephone, email, in person, chatting, Twitter and Facebook messaging, etc.)

•**Don't read in between the lines.** There is a lot of room for misunderstanding and misinterpretation with online communication. Reading in between the lines is making assumptions – and that's never a good idea.

•**Ask the hard questions** – you won't know unless you ask!

• **Ask more questions.** If you don't grasp what the other person is saying, nothing is wrong with asking more questions. If you find yourself not being able to communicate openly, beware of the tug of war. It may be a sign this is not the right person for you.

• **Look for the flow.** There is nothing better than a good flowing conversation, where one hour easily turns into three. Allow the pauses to be part of the conversation and don't be quick to fill the empty spaces. Ultimately, it should feel organic and unforced. If the conversation consistently doesn't feel natural or allows for you to be yourself, then move on.

Tip: Beware of the Tug of War

The physical game of tug of war is a favorite for many families at their reunions, and it was a go-to activity for my gym teacher in elementary school. He would divide our class into two teams, take out a very long and somewhat heavy rope that had a flag tied to the middle. The team that pulled the flag to their side would win. It was a very fun and intense activity with constant pulling, hence the name tug of war.

Tug of war as a game is fun, but in a conversation - it's exhausting.

When you find yourself constantly pulling and tugging to get the conversation flowing smoothly or for the other person to open up, take a moment to share how important communication is to you. Communication styles and expectations should be viewed in the same manner as chemistry, if not with more scrutiny. It's easy to understand the importance of chemistry because it's primal, it's physical, and it's either there or not. I would argue that communication should be held in the same regard, or you may have a major problem down the road.

Long term relationships and marriages will have a unique set of issues and obstacles to conquer. The ability to triumph over those obstacles rely on a commitment and good communication. Often successful relationships rely on a commitment *to* communicate, especially during rough times.

Do you really want to be with a person that you have to drag constantly to the gates of conversation? What will happen when your relationship encounters a major problem, or a minor problem becomes major because the communication isn't there? Beware of the tug of war, and don't feel responsible for doing the tugging. Effective communication is like the tango – it takes two.

A good way to remember the components of the Keep it Real Rule is to ask yourself the following questions:

• Does this friendship align with my goals and what I truly want?

• Will this allow me to be my true authentic self or does it require me to make unnecessary sacrificial changes to who I really am and the vision and goals I've set for my life?

• Am I communicating effectively with respect and in good taste?

{ 3 }

Getting Back in the Groove

A few years ago I recognized that dating had become something quite different from the last time I was on the dating scene. I had been divorced for eight years, and anyone could tell by my lack of dating experience that I was an online newbie. I remember feeling like a fish in a glass bowl, hesitating to press the save button after I would complete my profile. I wanted my profile to be a good representation of who I was and what I wanted at that particular moment in my life. It didn't take me long to realize that not everyone put as much time into their profile as I did.

The advice and recommendations I give in this guide are tips that I wish someone would have shared with me when I was getting back into the groove of things. Below are a list of recommended do's and don'ts when you're first getting started.

Do Limit the Number of Subscriptions

I recommend limiting your active subscriptions to no more than two dating sites at a time. Take the time to learn how each site functions. Dating sites will bombard you with profiles to view, and it will be easier to maneuver through the piles of mismatches if you limit yourself. It can save you money, time and will allow you to see if that particular site is a good fit.

Tip: Not All Dating Sites are Equal

Before you dive into purchasing a subscription, take advantage of the free memberships to see if you like the site and if online dating is the right avenue for you. Some people don't like the online dating experience, and that's OK. A poor experience could be due to a particular site you've joined. I recommend trying two to three different sites before you call it quits.

Some dating sites are like large dry deserts with hundreds of thirsty people wandering aimlessly in and out of chat rooms, only to find themselves stuck in an inbox.

Like many different kinds of life experiences, this is one that you may not receive what you put in, but you should still give it your all. One huge variable is the quality of the matches provided by the dating agency. You don't have any control over who gets sent to your inbox, but all other parts of the equation you do.

The truth is that you could meet a fantastic match at your next business conference, art class, while you're walking your dog, at the airport or your local grocery store. The dating site is just one avenue, and there are plenty of dating sites out there. Some sites score quite high on the raunchy scale while others are more sophisticated. Ultimately, it will depend on your taste, budget and preferences as to which site works best for you. Take your time and do your research.

Do Be Patient with the Process

I believe in being optimistic and having a positive outlook on life. However, I also believe in being realistic. The reality is, this can be a lengthy process, and the odds are that you will not meet your partner overnight or within your first few matches. If you let the process work, stay patient and positive, you will learn a lot about yourself and will become a better communicator along the way. It is normal to get excited about the first few matches – but hang in there. You never know – it could be match # 596 that is the one for you!

Do Respond

Call me old fashioned or simply smitten with old school mannerisms, but I think it's rude not to respond to messages or compliments from potential matches. If someone told you that you had pretty eyes in person, would you ignore them? Probably not. You may feel overwhelmed with winks, gifts and smiley faces at first, but many dating sites have auto responders that can help make this basic level of communication more efficient.

If you do not have an active or paid subscription, some sites will not allow you to communicate fully with members that have contacted you. It would be great if the dating site shared your subscription status so that people who wanted to communicate with you, were aware that you would not be able to respond. I suppose it's a way for the dating company to make money and to reel you into purchasing a subscription.

My advice is to respond when you can. I try to respond within 24 to 48 hours of receiving a message. However, I typically don't respond right away to requests to chat, especially if I don't know the person, or have not had the time to read their profile to determine if it's worthwhile.

Don't Be Your Alter Ego

Perhaps in a previous life, you were a talented, seductive, burlesque dancer. However, just because you woke up and decided to put on your super power undies, does not mean you should portray this side of yourself online. I'm sure there are plenty of people who would love to see your secret talent, but only a privileged few should get to know this side of you. Remember – it's all right to have fun, but keep in mind it's the internet. Be careful what you post!

Don't Hesitate to Hit "NO!"

As your inbox is being flooded with your daily matches, you may be thinking, no-no-no. Somewhere along the way, the auto feeder on your match-o-meter has missed a key piece of information from your profile, resulting in counts of different pictures with the same line, "Do you want to meet him? Yes, Maybe, No?"

After a sigh, a deep eye roll and an inner "hell no", you might as well help out the auto-feeder, and select the 'no' option. Hitting the 'no' button is not going to hurt anyone's feelings. Keep in mind, that as you are receiving those messages, somewhere your beautiful face is being sent to inboxes with the same options beneath it, and undoubtedly people are making their selections. So, keep it moving. Yes, Maybe, No? ... Next!

Don't Be Desperate

Loneliness is a real issue. With all of our busyness and over stimulated social networks, it's still possible to long for a deeper connection, and a partner to not only share the quiet moments, but to enjoy life. Perhaps one of the reasons you've decided to join a dating site is because you are lonely. No one ever talks about being lonely, but it's a part of life. Unfortunately, in our culture, this topic is somewhat taboo. I once heard someone say that loneliness is a choice. I don't know if I believe that, but I do believe it's possible to be in a room full of people and still feel alone. I'm not sure where you are on the spectrum of loneliness, but I know that it's possible to live a healthy and thriving life as a single person, and not experience the deep emotions of loneliness.

Nevertheless, if you are lonely, I encourage you NOT to make online communication decisions based out of loneliness. Predators can smell your loneliness through the network like a hound dog to red meat, and nothing good can come from you being desperate. You have to bring joy and happiness to the table of any friendship or relationship. It's too big of a burden to expect others to be your life source of energy – you will end up sucking people dry. You are valuable. Stay respectable and be patient. Don't cast your pearls so easily because you are starving socially and willing to accept an empty conversation for dinner.

Online dating should not be the pinnacle of your social existence. Try to find an interest to connect with people in your neighborhood or community. It is better to be alone than to be with the wrong person. Hang in there and hold on to your bearings. It will happen. Believe it.

{ 4 }

Catfishing

Catfishing has become somewhat of an internet phenomenon over the past few years. It's the dread of anyone who's online dating or have seen the television show or movie. The term 'Catfish' was the title of a 2010 documentary by Nev Shulman, who was in an online relationship with a woman he discovered was married and much older in age.

Catfishing in its most basic form is lying and pure deceit. In some cases, I would say, that catfishing is the intent to cause embarrassment and emotional pain to its victims. Catfishing happens when a person intentionally portrays themselves to be someone they are not. People who catfish are online predators. Use the following steps to avoid being caught in their nets.

Examples of "Hard Core" Catfishing

1.   A man portraying himself as a woman

2.   A woman portraying herself as a man

3.   A homosexual person portraying themselves as heterosexual

4.   Sexual orientation misrepresentation (Ex. A transvestite portraying himself as one gender and not disclosing his true nature; a Bi-sexual not disclosing sexual orientation.)

5.   A person that knows you personally but portrays themselves to be someone different. (Often to get revenge)

6.   A person that chooses a profile picture of someone else from the internet as their own

7.   A person that is married or in a relationship but is presenting themselves as being single

8.   A person that portrays themselves as a completely different race or ethnicity

How to Catch a Catfisher:

Below are five simple tools that can help you
Catch a Catfisher.

1.   **Google their Picture:** After you find out their real name – google them. Enter their name in several different search engines and see what type of images you find. If similar images pop up – then you have some assurance that you are talking to the right person. However, if you get a

completely different image on their Facebook page, or their tagged name comes up with vastly different images then you may have a Catfisher on your hands. To search an image, right click on the picture and save it to your desktop. Next, upload the photo to images.google.com. Delete the pictures from your computer after the search to avoid speed and space issues.

2.   **Get on a Video Call**: I can't say 100% that video calling will guarantee that you will not be catfished. People can be crazy and devise the most scandalous of plans, but it will help. If the person you are talking to does not want to video call, try to get to the root of why they are against video chatting and then make the decision to move on or not.

3.   **Greet & Meet**: After you come to the realization that you may have a meaningful connection, do not go more than 6 – 8 weeks without meeting that person. I realize that many online daters are matched with people from different cities and states. However, do your best to meet face-to-face. If the person gives you several excuses why they can't meet and cancels multiple times for a variety of 'emergencies', consider moving on. Your time is just as valuable. At most, this could be a Catfisher and at minimum, this person does not share the same value in meeting in person.

4.   **Get Verified**: Many dating sites have ID verification services that aim to verify the identification of its

members. In order to be verified, members give the dating site permission to access their social network accounts, such as Facebook, Twitter, LinkedIn, and Google+. The site is also able to verify your cell number by texting secure codes to your phone. If this is something you will require of your matches, then I recommend that you go through the process yourself to see how it works.

5.   **Go with your Gut**: If it looks like a duck, chats likes a duck, texts like a duck, refuses to video call like a duck, or meet in person – it's a duck! Go with your gut. This may sound weird since we are talking about online dating, but you can't make great decisions with your heart only. You have intelligence and a mind for a reason. Don't forget to use them.

Tip: Due Diligence is Your Responsibility

A year ago I was having a conversation about catfishing with a friend. We debated about who gets catfished more, men or women. During the conversation, he shared that he was tired of "thin beautiful faces being attached to over-weight bodies". At first I didn't know what to make of his comment, but after further explanation, he felt as if he was being catfished by women who he expected to weigh less or to be in better physical condition. I completely disagreed with him. My response was that catfishing is an intentional deception. This was not a case of intentional deception but rather, he never asked the right questions to determine if they shared the same fit lifestyle or valued the same level of physical fitness. If physical fitness is a deal breaker, then he should have kept it high on his priority list. Also, he could come to a plausible conclusion through basic questioning. My friend goes to the gym seven days a week. If she has a desk job, works out once per month and eats fast food for all major meals, then you may have a deal breaker on your hands! However, if you don't take the time to ask the right questions, respectfully and in good taste, you may get some unwanted surprises on your first date. Due diligence is your responsibility.

Photogenic Profiles

We all, will undoubtedly come across someone who takes good pictures. Their pictures are well angled with the perfect lighting, and captures their best side. However, we may be underwhelmed when we meet face-to-face. This is not a case of catfishing. Some people just take great pictures! On the other hand, if there is major photo editing being done, you can only blame yourself. You had the opportunity to video call, to see if they've been verified, and to conduct an image search prior to meeting them. Also, some people don't mind a little airbrushing on their pictures. Adjusting the lighting on a photo, is completely different then photo editing a super model's waistline into your picture. In tandem, some people are not photogenic at all and take horrible pictures. Don't completely rely on pictures to gauge attractiveness. Let the pictures be a starting point, and eventually video call or meet them in person.

Examples of Soft Catfishing (Misrepresentations)

1. Employment misrepresentations, such as saying you have a job, and you're actually unemployed. (Who's paying for dinner?)

2. Personality misrepresentations. (You're a very aggressive sexual person online but can't speak two complete sentences in person due to awkward social issues. Who are you? And should I be scared?)

3. Physical misrepresentations. (You communicate that you're a beach body but in real life you're a couch potato that enjoys watching workout videos on YouTube.)

"One drop of poison can spoil a whole glass of good pure water."

Think about it. Imagine a glass of the purest water on Earth. Add a single drop of poison to it. Would you drink it?

That little lie – that small, seemingly tiny misrepresentation, is that one drop of poison. If you wouldn't drink that glass of water, then you shouldn't poison the goodness of your profile with a drop of misrepresentation. The issue is simple. Misrepresentations distort the truth, create false expectations, and it's simply not fair to the person who's chugging it down.

Let's go back to the reason you decided to try online dating in the first place. Don't you want something true, real, and authentic? Well, in order to *receive* that, you have to first *be* that.

Be true.

Be real.

Be authentic.

These are the best rocks for a strong foundation in the most basic levels of friendship. Remember to keep it real.

Don't Worry – Be Prepared

As a newbie to online dating, you do not have to be the victim of catfishing. I don't want you to be so afraid of the possibility of being catfished, that you don't get back out there and try something new. Life is too short. Take the steps that I've outlined in this section and at the end of the day, trust your instincts. You have them for a reason!

{ 5 }

Safety First

You can never be too careful. As the saying goes – it's better to be safe than sorry. Below are a few safety tips that I have used throughout my online experience, and I have not been sorry for doing so.

Take Progressive Steps

Take progressive steps when engaging matches. Use the communication tools on the site, such as the chat and messaging apps before progressing to texting and telephone conversation. Giving out your personal information right away is never a good idea. Besides, what's the rush? Whenever a match is pressuring me to talk on the telephone, and I don't feel comfortable giving out my number at the time, my response is usually that I would like to get to know them a little bit better first. I ask if they wouldn't mind continuing the conversation via chat or messaging until I got more comfortable. This type of request is usually accepted and when it's not – it's OK.

Put em' in a Search Engine

A little due diligence can go a long way in establishing trust and providing yourself with a sense of security by simply putting their name in a search engine. You can also look them up on social networks such as Google+, Facebook, Twitter and LinkedIn. This isn't a safety issue, but it helps in verifying people are who they say they are. I also recommend putting your name in a search engine. When I searched my name, I discovered there is a porn star that is two letters from having my exact full name! I hope the matches who enter my name into a search engine spell it correctly. I wouldn't want there to be any unreasonable expectations.

Before the First Date

Never meet in person without first talking on the telephone or video calling. I make sure that I video call prior to my first date. Again, you want to know that you are talking to the right person, and it also helps with getting acquainted with the person and feeling more comfortable.

No Home Telephone

There doesn't seem to be very many people who have a home telephone these days but if you do, never give it out to your match until it's serious. Also, never place your home telephone number on your profile. Landlines are searchable online, especially if you haven't told your carrier, not to list you in online directories. It's very easy for people to find out where you live with your home telephone number. If you don't want the person to know your home address, then don't give them your home telephone number. Use your cellphone number instead.

No Small City Location Listings

If you live in a small city, do not enter your specific city location in your profile. I live in a small suburb of a major city. I use the big city as my location when setting up my profile. This will help in limiting unwanted and unknown matches from finding out where I live. It's easier to find your location when you live in a town of ten thousand versus a city of one million.

Online Dating Email Account

Use a separate email account for online dating that is different than your business or work email address. If you've ever been hacked or had your email spammed, I don't have to tell you the importance of taking even the smallest of cyber safety measures. It's also a good idea to keep your private life private, and having an extra email account will help.

Keep a Confidant

When going on your first couple of dates, get a confidant. Your confidant should be a person that you trust, who knows you well enough to have a few of your family contacts in case of an emergency. I recommend giving them your date's full name and the place and address of where you're going.

{6}

Deal Breakers

I'm sure that you've heard that it's never okay to talk about religion and politics in social settings. However, this is one situation in which that is not the case. If you are trying to meet the right person and sift through the hundreds of mismatches, it is important to establish a set of deal breakers.

Know Yourself

Before we can talk about deal breakers and preferences, you must first know who you are and what you want. If you are in your forties, I'm sure your outlook on life has changed since your twenties. Take a little time to think about what you want from this process and write it down. I'm not sure why, but there is something powerful about writing down your goals. You would be surprised how many people are on dating websites and don't know who they are, what they want and therefore, they are willing to settle for anything. When it comes to decision such as this a life, know yourself and don't apologize for wanting what you want.

What is a Deal Breaker?

If you search the word deal breaker online, you will see this word used in many different ways. Before I share my definition of a deal breaker and how it is used in the context of this book, I'll first let you know what a deal breaker is not. A deal breaker is not:

- A laundry list of pet peeves.
- An afterthought to bubbly conversation.
- A checklist to prove to yourself, that a break up with your current partner is looming in the near future.
- Old baggage packaged in the form of new rules.

A deal breaker is a set of predetermined uncompromising circumstances or values that you believe will inhibit the development of a lasting relationship.

These uncompromising circumstances should be discussed before you establish a meaningful connection, not afterwards. Also, I recommend that you have no more than a handful of deal breakers. If you end up with twenty to thirty deal breakers on your list, you either want to be alone for the rest of your life, or you will need to take the time to create a 3D avatar for a partner. You'll be waiting the rest of your life to find a perfection that doesn't exist in the real world. I recommend starting your list over and keeping it real!

Below are the common groups that your deal breakers may fall under:

- Chemistry / Sex Life
- Children / Family Planning
- Education & Employment
- Faith / Religion
- Finances
- Health/Wellness/Weight
- Lifestyle
- Pets/Animals
- Politics
- Social Habits: Smoking / Drinking
- Work/Life Balance Issues

Examples of Common Deal-Breakers

Remember, deal-breakers are absolutes, there's no wiggle room.

A person with small child/children

A person that has extreme political views (You can define extreme.)

A person that does not share core tenants of your faith

A person that doesn't share your view on social justice or environmental issues

A person that struggled with an addiction (ex. child porn, drugs, etc.)

A person that is extremely underweight or overweight

A person that works more than 60 hours per week (all work and no play.)

A person with a sketchy past (ex. criminal behavior, serial cheating, etc.)

Preferences

Preferences are not absolutes, but in a perfect world they represent your desired wants from your partner. For example, it's my preference to be with someone who doesn't have a pet. It's not a deal breaker if they own a pet, but I would prefer for my match to not have any pets or animals. However, if you own a small petting zoo in your backyard, consider yourself a pet rescuer or cat hoarder, that's completely different and that *is* a deal breaker. It's a deal breaker because now, we're talking about lifestyle differences. Another example is if you have severe allergic reactions to certain pets, and being around one causes you physical discomfort, this may be a deal breaker for you instead of a preference.

Shared Definitions

In addition to discussing deal breakers, as the connection progresses, I encourage you to discuss shared definitions of the commonly used words. People develop definitions that are based on their life experiences. For example, what does marriage mean to you? What does your idea of marriage look like on a daily or weekly basis? How do you express and receive love? How is your faith demonstrated? You want to know that when you say "marriage", "love", God", "faith", "family" that you share the same view, or at least know what these words mean to each other early on in the friendship.

Conversation Starters

Below are examples of questions you can ask to begin the deal breaker conversation. These questions were designed to spark a conversation, and often should be followed up with additional questions. These are just examples. The main idea is that you learn *how* the other person demonstrates these shared values in their everyday lives. Remember to listen and to share.

If **faith** is a high priority:

1.   Do you believe in God? What does God mean to you?

2.   How do you define your faith?

3.   What's the name of your church? How often do you attend?

4.   How is your faith expressed in your daily life?

5.   Do you have any expectations from your partner as it relates to your faith/religion?

6.   In what ways is the religion/faith you practice now, different from your religious experiences you had growing up?

If **family** is a high priority:

1.   Do you believe in traditional gender roles? If so, can you describe them? If not, why not?

2.   Do you want to have children (or more children)?

3.   What are your expectations for your partner as it relates to your children?

4.   What's your philosophy on child rearing or discipline?

5.   Can you tell me about your family? How important is your family's approval or acceptance of your partner?

6.   Is there anything about your childhood that you would change? If so, why?

If **finances** is a high priority:

1. What are your thoughts about household finances? Should they be shared?

2. Do you have a personal policy on lending money to family and friends?

3. What credit monitoring service do you use or recommend?

4. Do you have a favorite charity organization that you give contributions or donations to on a regular basis?

5. How do you envision yourself and lifestyle when you retire?

If **physical** fitness is your high priority:

1. How many times do you work out per week?

2. What's the name of the gym you belong to? How long have you been a member?

3. Is physical fitness high on your list of personal values? If so, how is this value demonstrated in your daily life?

4. What's your favorite type of exercise (biking, hiking, volleyball, lifting, yoga, running, etc.)?

5. How do you define "health & wellness"? (For some it's about healthy or "clean" eating, others exercise and for some it's more of a spiritual experience.)

Conversation Starter Example: This example is much better then asking for physical measurements or booty pictures.

"Health, wellness and physical fitness is very important to me and my lifestyle. I spend about 10 hours a week at the gym. I'm hoping to share this with my future partner. Can you share with me your view on health and wellness and if this is a significant part of your current lifestyle?"

General Questions: These questions don't necessarily link to a deal breaker, but they could provide more information about the person's values and serve as great conversation starters.

1. Are there any social or personal habits that you would consider a deal breaker?

2. When you're upset, how do you prefer to be communicated with?

3. How do you typically solve problems within a relationship?

4. What's your relationship like with your parents?

5. How many friends do you have? How would those friends describe you in three words?

6. What's a typical Saturday night like for you? Sunday afternoon?

7. Is there something you use to love doing (hobby) that you don't do anymore? Why?

8. What are you most passionate about?

9. Are there any instances where it's difficult for you to bite your tongue?

10. Is there a hobby or goal you look forward to achieving when you retire? Do you have a bucket list?

11. Are there any political views that you're hoping to have in common with your partner?

12. What values do you believe are required to sustain a long lasting relationship and to successfully weather life's storms?

13. What's the best vacation you ever had and why?

14. What is the best gift you've ever received and given? Why?

15. When you were a child, what did you want to be when you grew up?

The Profile Picture

Side view? Close up? Black and White? So many decisions. Certainly, this is a big part of your profile. It's the first thing potential matches will see. It's that three to five second decision, to click on your profile or not. I did not include photo tips in the Profile Helpers section because there's so much that can go wrong with profile pictures.

As discussed earlier, the Keep it Real Rule must be applied to your profile pictures and should represent the real you. The everyday you. Below are some tips on how to best present your profile picture.

Practice Taking Selfies

You don't have to purchase a professional headshot to post on your profile. The goal should be to put your best face forward. Practice taking a few selfies on your cell phone or laptop. Learn how to work your angles and don't feel weird about practicing. You can always delete the photos you don't like. Make sure you have good lighting, and the quality of the picture is not fuzzy or blurry. Some people prefer black and white photos, but I recommend a color photo for the main profile picture. If you prefer, you can include the black and white photo as a second picture.

Minimize Objects

I don't know how many times I've seen huge trucks in the forefront and little men in the background of profile pictures. I'm not saying the men were small in stature, but the scale of their profile picture was completely off. Perhaps these individuals were trying to convey their love for Tundra's, but when I have to squint to see you – it's a problem. Your main profile picture should be clear and display a good view of yourself. So make sure you are in your profile picture and ditch the objects!

Only You

Profile pictures with other women, men, children, parents, family, friends are very distracting, especially for your lead or main profile picture. Your main profile picture should have only you. Although may be the best big brother or Aunt ever, having your little sister or nephew in your profile picture leaves too much to the imagination for your potential match. Some dating sites will allow for you to caption your pictures. If you need to add these to your profile, I suggest making them your third or fourth picture with a simple caption such as, "#1 Big Bro" or "Best Aunt Ever". Usually there is a character limit to the captions, so keep them short and to the point.

Regarding children, I would not suggest having them on your main profile picture. There are other ways to convey that you are a package deal. Again, you can have your third or fourth picture be a family photo. Personally, I don't think it's wise to put individual images of children on dating sites or online. You can express that you're a proud parent with information in your profile description.

No Sunglasses

The eyes are the window to the soul. Why are you covering them up? Unless you have a medical eye condition that requires you to wear sunglasses, wearing them in your main profile picture is not a good idea. When you wear sunglasses, it sends a message that you are hiding something. You may be the most transparent individual, but the sunglasses may communicate something different to your potential match. Not everyone receives the "I'm-so-hot-and-super-cool" vibe that you're trying to send. Please take off the shades and smile. We want to see your eyes!

Every Day You

The main profile picture should represent the everyday you. If your match would see you on the street or in a restaurant, they should be able to recognize you. I've seen profile pictures, where men were playing golf, but golf was not listed as a favorite past time or anywhere else in their profile. It would have been better if these individuals captioned their photos with "Fave 2013 Vacation" or some-thing similar, which sends a different message rather that you're a golfer. In short, if you don't wear a three-piece suit or a tuxedo every day, keep it simple and make your main profile picture, the best every day you photo.

Six Months or Twenty Pounds

Here is where we must keep it real. I suggest that you change your profile picture every six months and if you have either gained or loss twenty or more pounds. I know, don't hate me - but it goes back to my Keep it Real Rule. If you don't want to update your profile picture because you've gained 25 pounds, then you have to think about it from your potential match point of view. It's a misrepresentation. You are portraying something different than you are in real life. The good thing with weight is that you can lose it just as you gained it. For those of you who want to gain weight, kudos to you, just update your profile picture, please.

I also recommend updating your main profile picture if you've have altered your appearance in any way. Such as changes to your hair color, if you've shaved your head, have become bald, grown a beard, had a facelift or other plastic surgery procedures.

For example, if you are naturally a brunette and decided to become a vibrant red head, change your profile picture with a caption that says "Loving my new look". If your other pictures have you as a brunette, this won't come as a shocker if you end up going on a date.

All of the tips listed above will help to manage expectations. If you love the changes you've made to yourself, then the right match will too – so no worries.

{8}

Profile Helpers

The very first profile I completed was on my cell phone. I had just come from having a fabulous girl's night out with a great group of friends, awesome pomegranate martinis and delicious conversation. I was feeling pretty good and got the sudden urge just to go for it! I had a BlackBerry at the time and decided to create my first profile on a very popular faith based dating site. I'm not sure if it was the martinis, but I ended up selecting that I was a WOMAN seeking a WOMAN between 45 and 50 years old. I am heterosexual and was in my early thirties at the time. Naturally, I didn't catch this mistake until I was completely done setting up my account. I started seeing profile pictures of women that I knew, pop up as potential matches. It was dreadful! Where were my sparkling red ruby slippers, so that I could click my heels three times and fix this mess? I was completely embarrassed. When I called the agency and spoke with the customer support representative, he told me it would take three business days to fix the problem. Three business days on a Friday night was actually five calendar days. For five days, I was matched with women who were ten to twenty years older than me. It got real weird when I saw one of my colleagues at work oddly posed in her car. Needless to say, I had a few OMG moments, but I have never created a profile on my cell phone again. I have only recently crossed over into the Android world, where there are apps, two way cameras and all kind of cool twenty first century features. If you do not have a newer smart phone, I recommend completing your profile on a laptop or computer, then downloading the mobile app and going from there.

Get your Headlines Together

People don't read. Let's face it, we live in a 140 character culture, and although the way that we communicate is moving faster than ever before, this has developed us to be a generation of skimmers. Even if you like to read, on many occasions we read until we get the gist of what we perceive is being communicated. Since this is our reality, your profile headline or the caption on your profile picture should effectively and succinctly communicate who you are and what you're looking for. This could be equated to an "elevator pitch" that is often talked about at business networking events. It can be witty and show your sense of humor. The goal is for your headline to reflect you, in as few words as possible.

Take the Test and Answer the Questions

Every dating site will have a unique compatibility tool that is used to help provide you with the best match possible. In general, you want to complete the quizzes or questionnaire so that you can experience better matches. Keep in mind, this will not guarantee better matches, it will just improve the probabilities. Some sites have very short compatibility features and others sites have hundreds of questions available to answer. Even so, take the quiz. It's worth it. I've been on quite of few different dating sites and after a while many of the questions are the same if not very similar. Even if the question says that it's "optional" – I recommend that you answer it.

Refine your Profile as Needed

Over time, your goals and desires may change. Perhaps you began this journey hoping to find your prince charming, but you've only encountered the frogs in the pond and now you're ready to lower your sights to finding a few points of compatibility with a travel buddy. I hope this is not the case. However, if your goals change, update your profile. You might also need to update your profile if you moved to a new location, if your family structure has changed, or if you had a lifestyle change. Whatever the case may be, I recommend updating your profile if any major changes have occurred in your life.

{ 9 }

More Pics Please

I asked a male friend why men always requested to see more pictures. He said "men are visual creatures – we need to see". I've heard this repeatedly since then, but women want to see too! The eagerness for the visual, should not overpower the requirement to be a gentlemen or a lady. Asking for additional pictures is not the problem. If you want to see more, you should ask to see more, but with respect and in good taste.

Respectful Requests

I remember the first time someone asked me for additional pictures. I was annoyed and a little confused. I'd taken the time to put, what I thought, was a good selection of photos on my profile page. More? Really? Exactly what do want to see? At that point, I'd never asked anyone for additional pictures, so why were they asking me? I've had men ask me for my measurements, and there was a number of guys who would ask me for pictures that were completely out of my comfort zone. Some of the requests were very offensive and would result in an automatic blocking of that individual. It seems as if some users get their adult entertainment accounts mixed up with their online dating memberships. Please don't confuse the two.

I recommend paying more attention to how members ask for additional photos. Some sites have made this simpler, by adding a button you can click. The site will make this request on your behalf. If I feel there's a meaningful connection, I'll send my Skype address to minimize any concerns. Remember to tailor all of your requests with respect and keep them in good taste.

The Real Reason

Let's get down to the nitty-gritty, shall we? What is the real reason you're requesting more pictures? On the other hand, what's the real reason you don't want to provide anymore?

If you are only interested in meeting a "friend" and this is your goal for going online, then keep it real and tailor your search preferences to people who are looking for the same thing. Don't try to connect with a person that is looking for long term relationship or marriage. If you do, you are not keeping it real, and you are wasting people's time.

Once it's out there – it's out there. Keep this in mind when you are obliging photo requests. You will be giving a lot of unearned trust to individuals who may only want to glance at your goods. Is it really worth it?

Be honest: I rarely speak to matches who wear hats and sunglasses on their profile pictures. But I kept getting messaged by this particular individual. He had a good profile, and we seemed compatible in many regards. I asked if he could send me a picture so that I could see his eyes and face. He messaged back and told me something that I've never forgotten;

"I am not a handsome man, but I am a good man. I am responsible, faithful, loving, caring with a good job and great heart. I hope that doesn't stop you from getting to know me."

A little vulnerability goes a long way and I couldn't say no after a reply like that. I welcomed his candor and friendship. Eventually, we had a video call, and the chemistry was not there, but - it ended up being one of my best online friendships.

Tip: Don't Rush to Judgment

This match lived only three hours away. That was a big deal because I'd just changed the location preferences on my profile, hoping to receive better matches. We had just gotten through our priority deal breakers and exchanged cell numbers. We both were working that day and planned to have our first telephone conversation later that evening. He sent me several endearing text messages throughout the day. I was feeling pretty good. That is until he sent me a text asking for more photos. I didn't understand. We had been communicating roughly three to four weeks. There were several photos on my profile page. I'd given him my real name and he could have put my photos or name into any search engine. I didn't understand what he wanted or what type of picture he was asking for. I didn't reply back right away. The pause in our texting put a halt to the flow of conversation.

The night before, I'd received several raunchy requests for "more pics". I was hoping this guy hadn't misled me. We had such a great connection with that point. I didn't want to say the wrong thing. I went back to work and sent him a text asking if he would rather Skype than talk over the telephone. As soon as I pressed the send button, I received a ridiculous text from him.

"I knew you were too good to be true. I've been catfished before. Delete me from your list of matches."

What the hell? Are you serious? I sat in my car stunned at what happened. I waited, but he never texted me back. He had been a catfish victim – I had no clue. Apparently, he still had some insecurities from the experience. Although I was upset, I felt kind of sorry for him. Both of our recent experiences had led us to draw the wrong conclusions about the request. I assumed he wanted naked pictures, and he assumed that I wasn't who I said I was. I took a moment to reply because now this fool had my real name and personal cell number. Even though, we had been communicating for a few weeks – he was still a stranger. My reply was short and to the point:

"It's apparent that you have some insecurities from your unfortunate experience. I have been genuine in all my exchanges with you. You're right – we're not a match! The next time you meet someone that you connect with, I hope you give her a chance. Otherwise, take some time to heal before you blow another potential friendship."

TaLisa Sheppard

In retrospect, we never should've had that conversation through text. I could have shared with him the type of photos other men were asking for, and he could have shared his catfishing experience. A little vulnerability on both of our parts would have led to a better understanding. Since this incident, I've grown not to be so bothered by requests for additional photos, and I regularly ask my matches if they've been catfished. Naturally, I was disappointed with this experience, but I was also grateful for the lesson I learned.

{ 10 }

Talk About It

Now that you have gotten beyond the profile picture, it's time to start communicating with your match. Communication is key to establishing good online friendships. Sometimes the distance that naturally exists in the online dating world can make it difficult to connect on an emotional level. Below are a few helpful tips in being an effective online communicator.

Read the Profile

A key part of good communication is listening. When it comes to online dating, listening is reading the profile. Although we live in a world of emoticons and limited characters, it's very important to thoroughly read the profile. The amount of detail a person has put into their profile may be an indication of how invested they are in the online dating process. Reading through the profile will also help to establish a starting point for conversation.

For example, if a certain education level is important to you, and you don't read the other person's profile to know they have a GED. That could make for an awkward conversation when you ask them which college they attended. Thoroughly reading the profile will help you gain insight into what they're looking for, including potential deal breakers.

Give em' the Digits

As the conversation progress, at some point you should want to give your match your telephone number. If you find yourself not wanting to give your personal number to someone, you need determine why you are still communicating with them. Be selective on who gets to talk to you on the telephone and who you give your cell number too. If you still have a landline telephone, I suggest only giving out your cell number. Some dating sites offer a private telephone numbers that you can purchase to communicate with members without giving them your personal cell phone number.

Don't Text About It

GM. LOL. SMH. WYD? BBFN. TYYL. GN. Geez. Not everyone is a fan of texting. Texting too much can be annoying. There is certainly a place for this type of immediate messaging, but trying to communicate about important issues via text is a not a good idea. There are certain things a telephone conversation can communicate that a text cannot. For example, fluctuations in the voice, pauses, background noises, answers in real-time, etc. Texting also leaves a lot for the other person to interpret, and this may not be the best choice since you are getting to know each other.

Although it seems like everyone, and their grandma are texting, there may be a generational gap with this method of communication. The twenty something's may prefer to text versus talk on the phone. However, if you are looking to establish a meaningful connection, don't rely on short cryptic messages to communicate with your potential partner. Take the time to talk on the telephone and eventually meet in person.

Get Tech Savvy

After you have thoroughly read through their profile, discussed your deal breakers, gave them your cell number and talked on the telephone, it may be time to meet the person online via video. Depending on your profile settings, the match may be distant and not necessarily live in your city or state. Before you take the leap to go out on a date, I recommend taking time to video chat. There are plenty of video applications, such as FaceTime, Skype, Google Hangout and Oovoo. Many of these video messaging services are free and have apps that can be downloaded on your cell phone.

Just as talking on the phone can provide better communication then texting, video calling can provide a deeper connection. On video, you get to see the eye rolling, the smiles, the laughter, gestures, fluttering of the eyes, and a host of other facial expressions and mannerisms which are important in communicating and making a connection.

THE GOAL IS TO FIND A WAY TO COMMUNICATE THAT WORKS BEST FOR THE BOTH OF YOU.

If you like to video call, but your match has a flip phone and only wants to talk on the telephone – well, someone will have to compromise. As long as you both are enjoying the conversations, having a good time getting to know one another, then you'll find a way to communicate that gives you both what you need.

{ 11 }

Sorry, We're Not a Match

I've said these words to a few good guys and it did not feel good at the time. I knew they had great hearts and I'd grown to respect them and their goals throughout our interactions. When you value your goals and like the person enough, to want what's best for them, you will find a way to break it off. It will only get harder as time goes on. Here are some pointers that will help.

Deal Breaker Prep

The deal breakers and list of compromises discussed in the previous chapter, will serve as a good basis for you to determine if this person is a good match and a contender to get to know on a deeper level. The deal breakers will keep you from making unnecessary connections with people that will not make the cut.

Don't Allow Yourself to Feel Bad

We waste precious time when we linger in online associations and relationships that we know will not work out. Don't allow yourself to feel bad when it's time to call it quits. When you feel there is not a connection, it's time to move on. The connection I am referring to is more than physical (although chemistry is very important) because often you may not have physically met the person yet.

The conversation will never be easy, but it gets easier over time. Especially as you become more comfortable with the process of meeting new people online and focusing on your compatibility needs.

Put Things in Perspective

One way that you can avoid feeling bad is to keep things in the right perspective. This is not a sprint, it's more like an Ironman marathon. You can stay grounded by sticking to the Keep it Real Rule, knowing your deal breakers, your dating goals, communicating effectively and consistently, and most importantly have fun.

Be Grateful

The suggestion to be grateful may seem odd, especially when you've just told someone that it's time to move on.

However, having a sense of gratitude will help you get closure and better process the encounter, no matter how brief. Perhaps you learned something new, or tried a different restaurant, or had a unique experience because this person crossed your path.

You can be grateful for a new or memorable experiences.

You can be grateful for how you've grown over the years. Perhaps several years ago, you wouldn't have been so brave and forward to express what was in your best interest.

You can be grateful for the inner peace you now have, for going with your intuition and letting this person go.

Gratitude is a choice.

Choosing to be grateful will help you put things in perspective, and better enjoy your online dating experience. Remember, this should only be a small part of your amazing life.

Saying Goodbye

If you have spent a significant amount of time getting to know someone, and you've decided they're not a match, refusing to call or text them back is not saying "Goodbye". Falling off the face of the Earth is cowardice and juvenile. This may be an acceptable way to end friendships in high school, but it's completely inappropriate for adults who are engaged in online dating. No one wants to have hurt feelings. But secretly hoping they may 'get the point', by refusing to communicate is offensive.

HOW YOU END THINGS MATTER. AFTER ALL, IT COSTS YOU NOTHING TO BE KIND.

Below are a few examples of how to end a friendship or online relationship cordially and respectfully:

1. "I don't think we're a match but I have appreciated the conversation. I wish you the best in your journey."

2. "You have a lot of good qualities that I'm looking for, but I have to be honest with myself, and I don't think we're a true match. I have enjoyed our great conversations and I wish you the very best. I know you will find that special someone."

3. "Thank you for liking my profile and for the email exchange. I don't think we're a match. I wish you all the best."

Remember, how you say things matter and how you end things matter. It often speaks volumes about your true character, not the character you *say* that you have, but the one that is exemplified by action.

On the Other End

No returned telephone calls? No replies to your text messages? Being let go can completely suck, but it's a part of this journey that you must accept. Unfortunately, I know from experience how difficult it is to move on, when the other person stops communicating for no apparent reason. When that happens – exhale and be grateful that you've dodged a bullet. They were not the kind of person you thought they were.

However, if a person takes the time to express to you, that you are not their match, and perhaps they "only want to be friends", do not start to campaign for their love or try to change their mind. Accept what they have to say, respect their decision and move on.

Also, don't feel the need to start a deep self-analysis when things don't work out. Sometimes, we may discover there are things in our life we should change if we want to be in a relationship. Those are lessons - not whipping lashes. Just like love, the 'like' factor has to be genuinely mutual. You can't make someone like or love you. Don't settle. You deserve to be liked and loved back.

{ 12 }

Enjoy the Journey

After you have experienced some ups and downs, it can be easy to forget to enjoy the journey. Whenever things start to become less than enjoyable, I recommend taking a break. The fun factor is important, and you can become fatigued and disengaged from an unsatisfactory online dating experience.

If you need to take a break, try unplugging for a day or two by turning off the notification alerts on your profile settings. Also, you can disable the automatic renewal on your account or cancel your subscription for a month or two. Trust me – the respite will be a breath of fresh air. When you're ready to go back online, you can renew your subscription or find a new site and start all over.

I've certainly had my share of disappointments and completely understand the ebb and flow of this type of online interaction. I've also had some wonderful experiences and have met interesting and good people along the way. It's a major reason I decided to write this guide and to share some of the lessons I've learned.

Stop looking for love? Yes. Instead, look for shared values, great character, good chemistry, compatibility and quality conversations. Hopefully this new approach will lead you to experiencing a few meaningful connections, and ultimately you finding a loving and lasting friendship.

It's been my objective to encourage you to stay true to your goal while making a minor adjustment in your focus. Remember to be safe, to ask the hard questions, to have fun, to move on, and to always keep it real. You are in control of your online dating experience, and whenever it starts to cause unhappiness and unwanted drama in your life, you can do something about it. It's your journey – enjoy it!

ABOUT THE AUTHOR

Actual Profile Picture

"Looking for my best friend."

TaLisa Sheppard is a romantic at heart, accountant by trade and entrepreneurial enthusiast. She is the author of several books including, *The Unexpected: An Unplanned Journey Through Choice, Do I Really Matter?* and *The Battle Breakers* series. TaLisa is a graduate of The Ohio State University. She is the former CFO of TWB Media Group and currently is the CEO of PMG Publishing House. More of TaLisa's works can be found on her website at www.talisasheppard.com.

www.ingramcontent.com/pod-product-compliance
Lightning Source LLC
Chambersburg PA
CBHW060534030426
42337CB00021B/4255